Capital Region Memories

A PICTORIAL HISTORY OF THE MID-1800s THROUGH THE 1930s

Capital Region Memories

A PICTORIAL HISTORY OF THE MID-1800s THROUGH THE 1930s

On the cover

FRONT COVER: The corner of State and Pearl Streets, Albany, circa 1920. See page 21.

BACK COVER: John Van der Veer (right), Belle Van der Veer, and an unidentified friend, 1910. See page 34.

INSIDE FRONT FLAP: Looking west up Washington Avenue from Albany City Hall as people dig out after the Blizzard of 1888. See page 84.

INSIDE BACK FLAP: Police officer in Albany, circa 1920. See page 76.

Photos curated by Kathryn Osterndorff and Caitlin Waite

Published by Pediment Publishing, a division of The Pediment Group, Inc. • www.pediment.com
Printed in the United States of America.

ACKNOWLEDGMENTS

The following organizations have contributed greatly to this project:

ALBANY INSTITUTE OF HISTORY & ART

 Albany Public Library
www.albanypubliclibrary.org

 BETHLEHEM HISTORICAL ASSOCIATION · ESTABLISHED · 1965

 BRUNSWICK HISTORICAL SOCIETY

 HOME OF THE LIME KILNS

 GLENVILLE History Center

GRAFTON HISTORICAL SOCIETY

 GREENBUSH HISTORICAL SOCIETY 1972

 RARITAN COEYMANS Historical Society

 HART CLUETT MUSEUM · HISTORIC RENSSELAER COUNTY

 HISTORIC CHERRY HILL · TURNING HISTORY UPSIDE DOWN

 THE LOUIS MILLER MUSEUM · HOOSICK TOWNSHIP HISTORICAL SOCIETY

 M.E. GRENANDER DEPARTMENT OF SPECIAL COLLECTIONS & ARCHIVES · UNIVERSITY AT ALBANY State University of New York

 NATIONAL · MUSEUM · OF RACING AND · HALL · OF · FAME

 New York State Archives

 Parks-Bentley Place Historical Society of Moreau & South Glens Falls

 PITTSTOWN BENS CO. N.Y. TOWN SEAL PITTSTOWN HISTORICAL SOCIETY

 THE SAND LAKE HISTORICAL SOCIETY · PRESERVING THE PAST · 1974

 SARATOGA SPRINGS PUBLIC LIBRARY

 SCHENECTADY COUNTY HISTORICAL SOCIETY

 STILLWATER PUBLIC LIBRARY

 TOWN OF PETERSBURGH NEW YORK 1791

 VILLAGE OF CASTLETON-ON-HUDSON NY

 VILLAGE OF NASSAU INCORPORATED

 Watervliet Historical Society

FOREWORD

In the early 1960s, a young Albany-raised journalist named William Kennedy was pursuing his career in Puerto Rico when he began to make a close study of a book self-published by a fellow *Times Union* staffer, a typographer named Morris Gerber, under the bare-bones title *Old Albany*.

Gerber's project would eventually grow into a four-volume series, drawing considerably on photos discarded by a long-gone *Times Union* librarian intent on culling the newspaper's files. As Kennedy would go on to write in his nonfiction history *O Albany!*, the Gerber tomes were "all zany books, lacking indexes or comprehensible organization and captioning." Zaniness aside, that's not too dissimilar from the volume you're holding right now: a collection of photos of Albany and its outlying neighborhoods from decades before, a period in which the river city grew into a center of commerce and a bustling hive of upstate life.

The Gerber books began to work on the imagination of Kennedy, who had just begun redirecting his considerable writing talent from journalism to fiction. They reminded him of the North Albany neighborhood where he had been born and raised, acting as "wonderful time machines for reentering the city that was." Eventually, they served as a handful of seeds for another series: novels by Kennedy forming what he called the Albany Cycle, an imaginary history of the region stretching from before the Civil War to the latter years of the Civil Rights movement. His fourth volume in that effort, *Ironweed*, won him the Pulitzer Prize in 1984.

All books—fiction or fact—can be time machines, catapulting the reader to other places and periods, and into the thoughts of people with whom we might not immediately feel kinship. We look at their faces as they stand in front of a storefront or home—either or both of which might well be disappeared from the built landscape for decades—and wonder what they're hopeful for, what they fear, what they're planning for dinner.

The images collected in this volume are meant to help us travel back, and remind us that the people who made the Capital Region their home more than a century before us grappled with all the things our generation has encountered, including global war, public health catastrophes, and technological upheaval.

This project owes a significant debt to the dogged work of the Capital Region's latter-day Morris Gerbers: people of the local historical societies and museums, large and small, organizations that increasingly find themselves struggling to stay afloat in an era of strained resources. Students of history—and if you're reading this, odds are you fall into that camp—would do well to seek them out and offer whatever support you can.

Kennedy, now past 90 and returned to the Capital Region for more than a half century, is still writing, still drawing an imaginary map of our community. We might hope that some new chronicler of our story will find in these pages the catalyst to embark on their own journey into the past.

Casey Seiler
Editor & Vice President, Times Union

TABLE OF CONTENTS

OPPOSITE: Glenville Highway Department's horse-drawn road scraper in front of Frank DeGraff's barn at the corner of West Glenville Road and Lover's Lane, Glenville, June 8, 1897. Reuben Smith, John Clapper, Benjamin Romeyn, William Clapper, and Charles A. Weatherwax are included.
COURTESY GLENVILLE HISTORY CENTER

chapter one

VIEWS AND STREET SCENES

It's not just the four seasons that can be found in the Capital Region (sometimes all on the same day, longtime residents like to joke), but various urban, rural, suburban, business, and residential sights and sounds—sometime all in the same city or town.

Rolling country roads cut through farmland and fields, while in the distance highway-encircled city skylines can be seen. Epic routes, centuries old, connect Albany to Saratoga and Schenectady to Troy, making stops at every village along the way. Roads follow the paths of the Hudson and Mohawk Rivers, clinging tightly to them before branching off to discover their own ways. People have always shopped and worked on streets like Broadway and Central Avenue and Union Street.

And everywhere people live, as they always have: in cozy homes on tree-lined boulevards, in streetside apartment buildings and tenements, high-rises and farms, cul-de-sacs and grand mansions.

The area is rich with Dutch influences owing to its early settlers, particularly in Albany. Simeon De Witt, Surveyor General of the State of New York, laid out a 1794 map of the city that created streets and avenues in a grid pattern, named for prominent local families: Ten Eyck to Van Schoick, Gansevoort to Ver Planck.

De Witt was also the man responsible for the flock of bird-calling names congregating in the heart of the city, Eagle and Hawk giving way to Swan, Lark, Dove, and Partridge, among others. Some of these streets eventually required avian updates, apparently, with Duck becoming Robin and Turkey morphing into Quail. Still others—Pigeon, Snipe, Sparrow, and Swallow—became altogether extinct, instead changing to Lake Avenue, Lexington Avenue, Ontario Street, and Knox Street, respectively.

Through all these changes as well as the ones brought by the evolution of travel—from horses to trains and streetcars to automobiles and highways—there are some constants, going as far back as De Witt and beyond. State Street in Albany still makes its majestic diagonal ascent to the State Capitol. The unchanged architecture of portions of downtown Troy still draws filmmakers there to recreate the past. Lush green spaces and natural wonders—the Helderbergs, the escarpment at Thacher Park, Congress Park and its casino, Central Park, Washington Park, and more—can make any of us immediate time travelers.

C.J. Lais

OPPOSITE: State Street in Albany, circa 1907. The State Capitol is visible in the distance. COURTESY LIBRARY OF CONGRESS / #LC-DIG-DET-4A22360

ABOVE: Congress Hall, Saratoga Springs, 1880. This was the second Congress Hall constructed on this spot, Gideon Putnam's original hotel having burned down in a fire in 1866. The new hotel, built in 1868, was constructed of brick and much grander than the last. It featured a courtyard, a large staircase in the lobby, 16-foot-high ceilings, and a ballroom connected to the hotel by an iron pedestrian bridge. The bridge, which had been made in Troy, passed over the unpaved Spring Street and allowed women to maintain their shoes and long dresses. COURTESY SARATOGA SPRINGS PUBLIC LIBRARY

ABOVE RIGHT: One of the earliest panoramic views of Troy by photographer James Irving, looking east from Congress Street toward Mount Ida, Troy, 1858. Identified in the background is the new Troy University, the site of Rensselaer Polytechnic Institute at the time of publication. COURTESY HART CLUETT MUSEUM

RIGHT: Delaware Turnpike in Clarksville, circa 1880. COURTESY CLARKSVILLE HISTORICAL SOCIETY

ABOVE: Businesses on Main Street in Coeymans, 1889.
COURTESY HARRY A. STURGES FOR RAVENA COEYMANS HISTORICAL SOCIETY

ABOVE LEFT: Collins House on the corner of Sixteenth Street and Broadway, one of seven hotels in Watervliet during the heyday of the Erie Canal, circa 1895. COURTESY WATERVLIET HISTORICAL SOCIETY

LEFT: Looking east down the north side of Hudson Avenue towards the Hudson River, Albany, 1900. Dean Street is on the left. The D&H Building (SUNY Plaza) stands in this spot at the time of publication. COURTESY ALBANY PUBLIC LIBRARY

ABOVE: Lake Drive, crossing the Tomhannock Reservoir (later to become New York State Route 7), Raymertown, early 1900s. COURTESY PITTSTOWN HISTORICAL SOCIETY

RIGHT: The south side of Sixteenth Street between Broadway and Second Avenue in Watervliet. The businesses visible in the photo are the Sansouci Theater (later became Family Theater) and Rowell Groceries and Meats. COURTESY WATERVLIET HISTORICAL SOCIETY

South Petersburgh looking north on what later became NYS Route 22, circa 1900. COURTESY TOWN OF PETERSBURGH

ABOVE: Looking down Jay Street towards State Street, Schenectady, circa 1900. The church in the background later became the site of the US Post Office.
COURTESY SCHENECTADY COUNTY HISTORICAL SOCIETY, NEW YORK HERITAGE DIGITAL COLLECTIONS

RIGHT: Two women helping a child cross a stream in Albany, circa 1900. COURTESY HISTORIC CHERRY HILL

ABOVE: State Street and Broadway in Albany, after 1869. The building on the corner, that had previously housed the well-known Albany Museum, was erected in 1831, expanded, and remodeled after an 1861 fire.
COURTESY ALBANY PUBLIC LIBRARY

ABOVE LEFT: Marion Miller on Main Street in Stillwater, circa 1900.
COURTESY STILLWATER PUBLIC LIBRARY AND THE HISTORIAN'S OFFICE

LEFT: Village of South Petersburgh looking east, circa 1900. The large building in the foreground was a tavern built by War of 1812 veteran Aaron Worthington. It burned on April 13, 1921. COURTESY TOWN OF PETERSBURGH

ABOVE: North Main Street (later became Hudson Avenue) in Stillwater, early 1900s.
COURTESY STILLWATER PUBLIC LIBRARY AND THE HISTORIAN'S OFFICE

ABOVE RIGHT: Looking up Broadway in Saratoga, circa 1903. COURTESY NEW YORK STATE ARCHIVES

OPPOSITE: Broadway at the United States Hotel, Saratoga Springs, circa 1907.
COURTESY LIBRARY OF CONGRESS / #LC-DIG-DET-4A27640

RIGHT: Looking toward Eagle Mills from McChesney Avenue Extension, Brunswick, circa 1915.
COURTESY BRUNSWICK HISTORICAL SOCIETY

ABOVE: Houghtaling Farm at Bennett Hill in Clarksville, circa 1910. COURTESY CLARKSVILLE HISTORICAL SOCIETY

RIGHT: Village of Grafton as seen from NYS Route 2, 1908. COURTESY GRAFTON HISTORICAL SOCIETY

ABOVE: Alplaus Creek, Alplaus, Schenectady County, 1910.
COURTESY GLENVILLE HISTORY CENTER

ABOVE LEFT: Brick Church Road at the intersection of Route 7 and Route 278, Brunswick, circa 1910. Gilead Lutheran Church can be seen on the hill at right. COURTESY BRUNSWICK HISTORICAL SOCIETY

LEFT: State Street, Schenectady, circa 1909. The Orpheum Theater and the Wallace Company can be seen. The Orpheum was renamed The Palace Theatre in 1918, and again in 1923 to Strand Theatre. It was notable for being the first Schenectady movie house to screen a "talking picture." Al Johnson's "The Jazz Singer" was shown there in December of 1927. The Wallace Co. building was constructed in 1892 and expanded in 1910. The company was a downtown mainstay until its closure in 1973.
COURTESY SCHENECTADY COUNTY HISTORICAL SOCIETY, NEW YORK HERITAGE DIGITAL COLLECTIONS

LEFT: Looking down the south side of State Street east of Broadway in Albany, 1914. The D&H Building (SUNY Plaza) stands in this spot at the time of publication. A large sign on the side of the building on the corner says: "Read the Knickerbocker Press." COURTESY ALBANY PUBLIC LIBRARY

OPPOSITE TOP: Overlooking the riverfront at the foot of State Street from the Albany Yacht Club, 1911. One of America's oldest yacht clubs, the Albany Yacht Club was first organized in 1897, and had numerous locations along the original waterfront. In 1903 the yacht club moved to a new home on the pier. The club had its last meeting in this location on September 11, 1911. COURTESY NEW YORK STATE ARCHIVES

OPPOSITE BOTTOM LEFT: Dedication Parade for the State Education Building in Albany, 1912. COURTESY NEW YORK STATE ARCHIVES

OPPOSITE BOTTOM RIGHT: Looking down the south side of State Street toward Broadway, Albany, 1917. COURTESY ALBANY INSTITUTE OF HISTORY & ART

ABOVE: Train at State Street railroad crossing, Schenectady, 1905. Despite the vigilance of crossing guards, people and horses were killed regularly each year at the State Street and Liberty Street crossings. Overhead railroad crossings were started in the spring of 1905, and completed toward the latter part of 1907. COURTESY SCHENECTADY COUNTY HISTORICAL SOCIETY, NEW YORK HERITAGE DIGITAL COLLECTIONS

ABOVE LEFT: State Street and Broadway, Albany, 1918. COURTESY ALBANY INSTITUTE OF HISTORY & ART

OPPOSITE: Corner of Erie Boulevard and Nott Terrace, Schenectady, 1917. COURTESY SCHENECTADY COUNTY HISTORICAL SOCIETY, NEW YORK HERITAGE DIGITAL COLLECTIONS

LEFT: The corner of State and Pearl Streets, Albany, circa 1920. COURTESY ALBANY INSTITUTE OF HISTORY & ART

ABOVE: USS *Los Angeles* dirigible flying over downtown and the SUNY Plaza building in Albany on February 22, 1931. COURTESY TIMES UNION HISTORIC IMAGES

ABOVE RIGHT: Clums Corners in Brunswick, 1920. The road heading left is Route 278, straight ahead is Tamarac Road, and to the right is Route 2. The men at left are standing in front of Clums Blacksmith Shop. COURTESY BRUNSWICK HISTORICAL SOCIETY

OPPOSITE TOP: Overlooking the Plaza at Broadway in Albany, circa 1935. COURTESY ALBANY PUBLIC LIBRARY

OPPOSITE BOTTOM RIGHT: Route 43 East in West Sand Lake, circa 1935. COURTESY SAND LAKE HISTORICAL SOCIETY

OPPOSITE BOTTOM LEFT: *Albany Evening News* & *Knickerbocker Press* promotion featuring an overhead view of New York, January 1936. COURTESY TIMES UNION HISTORIC IMAGES

RIGHT: North Ferry Street Bridge over the Erie Canal, Albany, circa 1925. COURTESY ALBANY INSTITUTE OF HISTORY & ART

THE KNICKERBOCKER PRESS

LEHMAN URGES HIGHER LIQUOR TAXES TO FINANCE SOCIAL SECURITY IN STATE

chapter two

TRANSPORTATION

Hear that sound? That's the sound of progress. Maybe it's the clomp of horses' hooves on a woodplank turnpike. Or the whistle of a train leaving the West Albany rail yards. The electric hum of the trolley cables, or the chop of an airplane propeller.

Ever since Henry Hudson's ship made its journey up "the river that flowed both ways," as Native Americans described it, our region's development has been shaped by transportation—the roads and rails that linked our cities, and the innovations that made it possible to reach farther, get there faster, imagine more.

The Erie Canal, opened in 1825, was a triumph of vision, engineering, and sheer muscle. Stretching more than 360 miles from Albany to Buffalo, it connected the Great Lakes to the Atlantic Ocean and beckoned settlers into the Mohawk Valley and beyond. The canal system cemented New York's place as a leader in commerce and industry—and our region's position as a key player in both realms during the early decades of our nation.

But that's just one entry on our roster of transportation milestones. New York's first passenger rail journey? Albany to Schenectady, 1831. The first long-distance flight between two US cities? Aviation pioneer Glenn Curtiss flew from Albany to New York City in 1910. The United States' first municipal airport? Yep, that would be Albany.

And as a center for industry, the Capital Region helped propel the nation's story forward. Consider the Jupiter, a steam locomotive built in Schenectady: It was one of the two engines that met up at Promontory Summit, Utah, in 1869, where they drove in the golden spike and completed the Transcontinental Railroad. And Engine 999, built at New York Central Railroad's Albany yards: It topped 100 miles per hour in 1893 and set a world record as the fastest land vehicle.

From the steamboats that churned up the Hudson from New York City to the automobiles that reshaped the Capital Region—and forever changed American life—here's a look back at how we used to get around.

Akum Norder

OPPOSITE: Tugboat *Lillian* on Canal at Mechanicville, circa 1907. COURTESY ALBANY INSTITUTE OF HISTORY & ART

RIGHT: Troy-West Troy Ferry, Watervliet. Before the construction of the Congress Street Bridge in the 1870s there were ferries that ran between Troy and West Troy at Ferry Street (later became Sixteenth Street), Fourteenth Street, and Twenty-Third Street.
COURTESY WATERVLIET HISTORICAL SOCIETY

BELOW RIGHT: Construction work on the Erie Canal in Scotia, circa 1895.
COURTESY SCHENECTADY COUNTY HISTORICAL SOCIETY, NEW YORK HERITAGE DIGITAL COLLECTIONS

BELOW: Carriage leaving Glens Falls for Lake George, 1870.
COURTESY HISTORIC CHERRY HILL

ABOVE: Day Boat *New York* on the Hudson River approaching Albany, 1900. COURTESY ALBANY PUBLIC LIBRARY

ABOVE LEFT: The Hudson River Day Line steamer *Albany* passing Baeren Island and the Knickerbocker Ice house in Coeymans, circa 1890s. The *Albany* operated from 1880–1930. COURTESY HARRY A. STURGES FOR RAVENA COEYMANS HISTORICAL SOCIETY

LEFT: *Frank A. Jagger* canal boat, Albany, circa 1875. Aside from being a graduate of Union College and an avid reader, Jagger was best known for his work in the Albany lumber business, as evidenced by an obituary in the *New York Lumber Trade Journal* three days after his passing, "Mr. Jagger was the *Journal*'s news representative, and in this capacity he was in close touch with all the dealers at all times and had, as a result, a wonderful store of trade history and anecdote. He witnessed the passing of the district's men of another generation and saw new ones take their places in the famous lumber market of the State capital. The news of his death was a shock to the entire trade, whose respect and confidence he held to a high degree." COURTESY ALBANY INSTITUTE OF HISTORY & ART

ABOVE: Express delivery wagon for the Charles A. Crape Cash Store in Sand Lake, circa 1895. COURTESY SAND LAKE HISTORICAL SOCIETY

OPPOSITE: The engineer and fireman posing alongside Adirondack Railway engine No. 2 in Glenville, 1895. COURTESY GLENVILLE HISTORY CENTER

RIGHT: Eagle Mills Creamery delivery wagons outside the creamery on Moonlawn Road in Brunswick, 1897. The business was owned by Lewis Thurston. The 1905 state census lists Thurston's occupation as that of manager of a butter factory. The old creamery serves as home to Bob and Becky Cipperly at the time of publication, who have lived there for around 50 years. In 2016 they were presented with a bronze historic building marker by the Brunswick Historical Society. COURTESY BRUNSWICK HISTORICAL SOCIETY

BELOW RIGHT: Elmer Phillips driving hay wagon, Austin Road, Pittstown, circa 1910. COURTESY PITTSTOWN HISTORICAL SOCIETY

BELOW: Three children in a horse cart in front of Grafton House, Grafton, circa 1895. COURTESY GRAFTON HISTORICAL SOCIETY

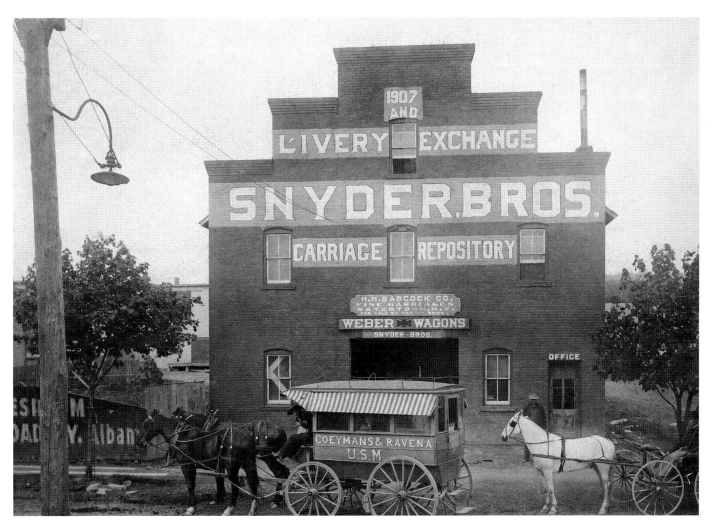

ABOVE: Champlain Canal, Stillwater, circa 1900.
COURTESY STILLWATER PUBLIC LIBRARY AND THE HISTORIAN'S OFFICE

ABOVE LEFT: Delivery wagon for John Hilton & Co. Grocers at 1417 Broadway in Watervliet. Standing at front is John Thomas Connell.
COURTESY WATERVLIET HISTORICAL SOCIETY

LEFT: A US Mail wagon in front of the Snyder Brothers Livery on Railroad Avenue, Ravena, circa 1900. The building was erected in 1907 for use as a livery and a carriage repository. They sold horse-related necessities, as well as wagons and carriages of all sizes and descriptions. The Snyder Brothers also provided residents transportation to and from the railroad station, ran the Ravena-Westerlo stage coach business that carried passengers and the Mail, and operated a passenger service to and from Albany (sometimes by sled). With the emergence of the automobile, they built a garage in 1914, located on Main Street next to the Odd Fellows Temple. COURTESY HARRY A. STURGES FOR RAVENA COEYMANS HISTORICAL SOCIETY

ABOVE: Leland Bennett and a woman identified as Miss Fahey seated on the ground with an automobile tire and inner tube, Glenville, 1905. COURTESY GLENVILLE HISTORY CENTER

OPPOSITE: One of the first Cadillacs purchased in Glenville, 1905. COURTESY GLENVILLE HISTORY CENTER

ABOVE: Troy and New England Railway, circa 1900. The rail line ran from Albia in Troy to Averill Park in the Town of Sand Lake, from 1895–1925, bringing visitors to the many lakes that were located in Sand Lake. COURTESY HART CLUETT MUSEUM

ABOVE RIGHT: Lincoln Spring Company wagon, Saratoga Springs, circa 1905. Between 1896 and 1910, Lincoln Spring Company and the Natural Carbonic Gas Company drilled hundreds of feet down into what would become known as the Lincoln Springs. They extracted carbon dioxide gas, in demand due to the popularity of soda fountains. When water levels began to recede, the state was forced to intervene, closing the large gas extraction companies and establishing the State Reservation at Saratoga Springs (later Saratoga Spa State Park) in 1911. In 1915, the Lincoln Baths were opened in a wooden structure built from a closed extraction company, utilizing the water's gas bubbles for therapy in the baths. Although the original bathhouse was destroyed in a fire in 1927, a new building was erected two years later made of stone, steel, terra-cotta, and concrete. It stands at the time of publication at the entrance to Spa State Park. COURTESY SARATOGA SPRINGS PUBLIC LIBRARY

RIGHT: John Van der Veer (right), Belle Van der Veer, and an unidentified friend on Cranes Hollow Road, West Glenville, 1910. COURTESY GLENVILLE HISTORY CENTER

LEFT: The lower bridge over the Little Hoosic River in South Petersburgh, circa 1912. Originally a wooden covered bridge, it was destroyed by fire in 1911 and almost immediately replaced by structure shown here. At one point it had the distinction of being the longest concrete arch in Rensselaer County. COURTESY TOWN OF PETERSBURGH

BELOW LEFT: The Troy-to-Grafton bus on April 10, 1910. Identified in the photo are John Burdick and his wife Louise. COURTESY GRAFTON HISTORICAL SOCIETY

ABOVE: Petersburgh train station, circa 1905. The railroad was late in coming to the Little Hoosick Valley. It was not until 1869 that a line was opened between Chatham, New York, and Bennington, Vermont. Because of its serpentine route, it was known as the "Corkscrew Line." COURTESY TOWN OF PETERSBURGH

RIGHT: United States Shirt and Collar Company in Stillwater, circa 1915. Michael F. VanVranken is identified second from left.
COURTESY STILLWATER PUBLIC LIBRARY AND THE HISTORIAN'S OFFICE

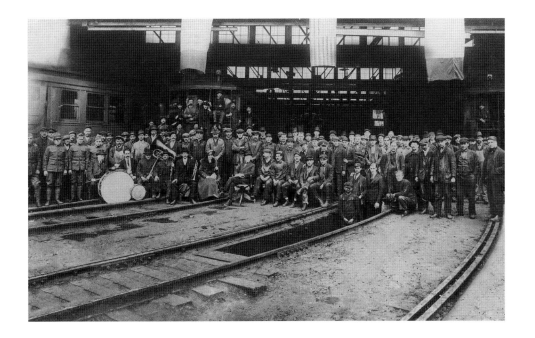

ABOVE: Steamboat *Dean Richmond*, late 1800s. Built in 1865 and scrapped in 1909, the steamer met with its fair share of disaster in its 44 years on the water. In 1867 the *Richmond* was in a collision when a miscommunication caused the Troy night boat *C. Vanderbilt* to run into the port side of the ship, causing it to sink and leaving a porter dead. After being raised and repaired, the *Richmond* was placed back in service on the night line. Another accident happened in 1877, leaving no injuries but causing thousands of dollars of damage to the engine of the vessel. COURTESY ALBANY PUBLIC LIBRARY

ABOVE LEFT: American Locomotive Company (ALCO) employees posing with soldiers in Schenectady, circa 1918. The American Locomotive Company was created in 1901 with the merger of several smaller companies, making it the second largest manufacturer of steam locomotives in the United States. COURTESY SCHENECTADY COUNTY HISTORICAL SOCIETY

LEFT: Stillwater Trolley workers in 1919. Identified in the photo: Chester Bloomingdale, Rodney Hickey, Bernard Osgood, Denny Roberts, John Collamer. COURTESY STILLWATER PUBLIC LIBRARY AND THE HISTORIAN'S OFFICE

ABOVE: Taxi drivers outside Clum's Hotel in Averill Park, circa 1925. COURTESY SAND LAKE HISTORICAL SOCIETY

OPPOSITE: Operators Edwin Haight and Frank Sherman at the telegraph office of the Ravena Railroad Station, circa 1925.
COURTESY HARRY A. STURGES FOR RAVENA COEYMANS HISTORICAL SOCIETY

RIGHT: Women from Nassau's Grace Methodist Church getting ready to take a bus trip to Albany, circa 1935. Once the trolley line went out of service in 1929, United Traction Company bus service replaced the route. COURTESY VILLAGE OF NASSAU

BELOW: Schenectady County Airport, Glenville, 1930. It has been speculated that this photo was taken during a visit by Charles A. Lindbergh following his transatlantic flight in 1927. COURTESY GLENVILLE HISTORY CENTER

Opening day on the Stillwater Bridge, 1931.

chapter three

COMMERCE AND INDUSTRY

"The Collar City." "The Spindle City." "The City that Lights and Hauls the World." Here in the Capital Region, we have long defined ourselves by the things we make. Industry runs through our history like the rivers that shape our communities—and those rivers were one of the reasons for our region's longtime industrial strength. The Mohawk and Hudson, along with their many tributaries, powered the water wheels that turned the belts and gears of early 19th-century factories, and turned us into a major US manufacturing center.

Water power wasn't our only advantage. We also had innovators like Scottish-born Henry Burden of Troy, who invented a horseshoe-making machine that could turn out a shoe every second; Albany's John Wesley Hyatt, who created the first commercially viable plastic and founded the Albany Billiard Ball Company; and Hannah Lord Montague, credited with coming up with the idea for detachable shirt collars and cuffs, launching an industry that came to define her city of Troy. And don't forget Thomas Edison, who came to Schenectady in the 1880s with his Edison Machine Works—the company that became General Electric.

We had skilled laborers, many of them immigrants, who provided the muscle and the know-how—and, in time, the determination and courage to demand better pay and working conditions and spur on the development of the labor movement.

And we had that most essential of assets: location. The Capital Region, at the confluence of two rivers, has always been a crossroads. Our well-established transportation network—canals, then rail, then good roads—gave us access to markets south in New York City, east in New England, and out into America's developing west. This network brought in raw materials like trees and pig iron and sent them out as finished lumber and paper and horseshoes and stoves.

From the factories that fueled the region's growth to the small shops and family businesses that build community, we have reason to be proud of our legacy of work.

Akum Norder

....

OPPOSITE: Washing, filling, and crowning bottles at a mineral water bottling plant run by the New York State Conservation Commission in the New York State Reservation (later became Saratoga Spa State Park) near Saratoga Springs, 1918. COURTESY NEW YORK STATE ARCHIVES

ABOVE: Walter A. Wood Mowing and Reaping Machine Company workers on the John Street Bridge in Hoosick Township, circa 1868. The bridge washed out in a flood and was rebuilt in the 1870s. COURTESY HOOSICK TOWNSHIP HISTORICAL SOCIETY

ABOVE RIGHT: White's Meat Market on the corner of Church and John Streets in Hoosick Township, circa 1860. One of the longest running businesses in the village, White's Market opened its doors around 1850 and stayed in business until 1927. It first sold fresh meats, fruits, and vegetables, and later expanded into carriages. COURTESY HOOSICK TOWNSHIP HISTORICAL SOCIETY

RIGHT: Workers in the Walter A. Wood Mowing and Reaping Machine Company in Hoosick Township, circa 1885. Wood worked as a blacksmith and a machinist before purchasing shop rights to a reaper patented by John Manny of Illinois in 1852. Wood went into business manufacturing reapers, producing only two his first year. He continued to improve the design of his farm implements, and by the 1860s he was winning awards and capturing worldwide attention for his machines. The Walter A. Wood Mowing and Reaping Machine Company went public in 1866, and production and sales rose considerably. By 1884, Wood's factory had produced a total of 500,000 machines and had a workforce of 2,000 employees. COURTESY HOOSICK TOWNSHIP HISTORICAL SOCIETY

LEFT: W. M. Whitney & Co. dry goods store at 43–49 North Pearl Street, Albany, circa 1885. The store was on the east side of the street, between Steuben Street and Maiden Lane. William M. Whitney came to Albany in the early 1860s and bought into the dry goods business, becoming the head in about 1866. The store—which by the '30s had become Whitney's Department Store—sponsored a Christmas Parade from the late 1930s until 1966, with a hiatus in World War II. The parade always made its way down State Street and Pearl, drawing thousands to watch the festivities and visit with Santa at Whitney's Toyland.
COURTESY ALBANY PUBLIC LIBRARY

ABOVE: T. F. Toohey, 39 South Pearl Street, Albany, 1886. COURTESY ALBANY INSTITUTE OF HISTORY & ART

ABOVE RIGHT: White Sewing Machine and Bicycle Company, 92 North Pearl Street, circa 1895. COURTESY ALBANY INSTITUTE OF HISTORY & ART

RIGHT: Factory workers, Village of Castleton-on-Hudson, circa 1890.
COURTESY VILLAGE OF CASTLETON-ON-HUDSON

LEFT: Fort Orange Paper Co. press room workers, Village of Castleton-on-Hudson, circa 1890. Opened in 1856 by Charles Benthuysen, the paper mill was purchased by Woolworth & Graham in 1881, who called it the Fort Orange Paper Company. The mill produced postcards, bank books, colored paper, pads, and tablets at a rate of 16 tons per day. By 1895 about 200 men were employed at the mill.
COURTESY VILLAGE OF CASTLETON-ON-HUDSON

BELOW LEFT: A. Mendleson and Sons employees, 1895.
COURTESY STEPHANIE WACHOLDER AND IRA MENDLESON III

BELOW: Baldwin's Ice Plant in North Hoosick, the largest supplier of ice to the Village of Hoosick Falls, circa 1890.
COURTESY HOOSICK TOWNSHIP HISTORICAL SOCIETY

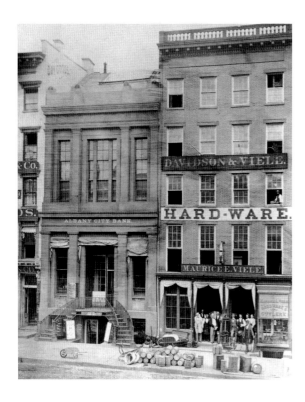

ABOVE: Businesses on the north side of State Street, between James Street and Broadway in Albany, circa 1850. Visible in the photo are Albany City Bank and Davidson & Viele Hardware. COURTESY ALBANY PUBLIC LIBRARY

ABOVE RIGHT: Jay Lamphere, Unk, and Ruben Lamphere at Rubens Saw Mill on the corner of Forest Lake Road and Cranberry Lake Road, Grafton, circa 1895.
COURTESY GRAFTON HISTORICAL SOCIETY

BELOW RIGHT: Petersburgh Creamery, circa 1895. On the other side of the lower bridge in South Petersburgh was a creamery where local farmers could bring their milk to have the cream separated out. The cream was then sold to processors to make cheese and other products. The creamery ceased operations in 1920. COURTESY TOWN OF PETERSBURGH

ABOVE: Ketchums Store, Wynantskill, North Greenbush, circa 1895. COURTESY GREENBUSH HISTORICAL SOCIETY

TOP: Albany Billiard Factory, circa 1900. COURTESY ALBANY INSTITUTE OF HISTORY & ART

LEFT: Employees of the Winters Brothers Pork Packing Company on Elm Street in Nassau displaying the tools of their trade, circa 1895. First established in the 1870s, the company's products were sold throughout the Capital District. COURTESY VILLAGE OF NASSAU

RIGHT: Workers in a collar shop located over a store in Raymertown, circa 1900. COURTESY PITTSTOWN HISTORICAL SOCIETY

BELOW RIGHT: Storefront of Abel & Brown, a hardware and appliance store on Classic Street in downtown Hoosick Falls, circa 1900. COURTESY HOOSICK TOWNSHIP HISTORICAL SOCIETY

BELOW: Work crew posing with power plant equipment during the construction of the Spier Falls Dam circa 1901. In spring 1901, the Hudson River Electric Company was organized "to construct dams on the Hudson in Saratoga, Warren, and Washington Counties," and their first endeavor was the dam at Spier Falls. Ironically, although one of the goals in the company's dam building enterprise was public safety by way of flood control, the construction at Spier Falls resulted in the death of at least 29 workers. At the time of its completion in 1903, the Spier Falls Dam was the fourth largest dam in the country, measuring 1,800 feet long and 100 feet high. COURTESY PARKS-BENTLEY PLACE, HISTORICAL SOCIETY OF MOREAU AND SOUTH GLENS FALLS

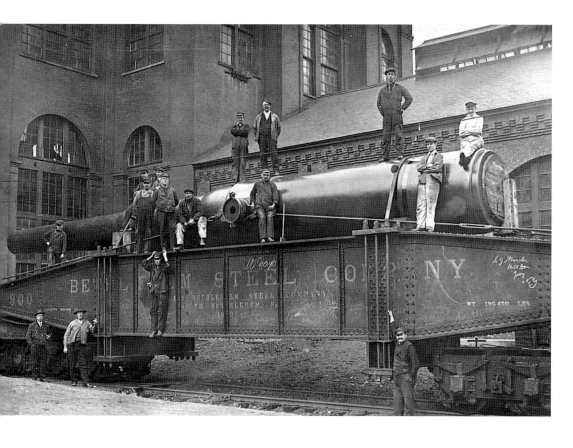

ABOVE: Glass Lake Hotel, Sand Lake, circa 1900. COURTESY SAND LAKE HISTORICAL SOCIETY

ABOVE LEFT: Large gun ready to ship from Bethlehem Steel Company, Troy, circa 1900. The earliest direct predecessor of Bethlehem Steel was the Bethlehem Iron Company, a producer of railroad rails that began manufacturing ordnance and armor plate in the 1880s. As a result of their expansion, a new Bethlehem Steel Company was incorporated in 1899 and leased all the property of the Bethlehem Iron Company. They purchased all assets on August 16, 1901.
COURTESY WATERVLIET HISTORICAL SOCIETY

BELOW LEFT: American Locomotive Works at Schenectady, circa 1905.
COURTESY NEW YORK STATE ARCHIVES

ABOVE: Workers at a sawmill on the corner of Austin and Gifford Roads in Pittstown. Severe Bellard identified in the front row. COURTESY PITTSTOWN HISTORICAL SOCIETY

OPPOSITE: Business owners in front of the Almeron Roberts Building on the corner of Main Street and Pulver Avenue in Ravena, circa 1905. From left: Fred Baldwin, John Babcock, George W. Babcock, Almeron Roberts.
COURTESY HARRY A. STURGES FOR RAVENA COEYMANS HISTORICAL SOCIETY

Market in Stillwater, circa 1905. COURTESY STILLWATER PUBLIC LIBRARY AND THE HISTORIAN'S OFFICE

An advertisement for General Electric in Schenectady featuring electric heating and cooking appliances, December 26, 1908. Appliances being advertised included a toaster, a samovar, and an egg cooker.

ABOVE: Local businessmen behind the tailor shop at 105 Madison Avenue in Albany, circa 1907. Identified in the photo are George Farinacci (second from left) and John Virgilio (far right). COURTESY ALBANY INSTITUTE OF HISTORY & ART

ABOVE RIGHT: Newsboys in Schenectady, February 1910.
COURTESY LIBRARY OF CONGRESS / #LC-DIG-NCLC-03458

OPPOSITE: The public market on the Lyon Block in Albany, 1913. The tower of the since demolished First Methodist Church and entrance to the former First Baptist Church can be seen at left. The twin spires of the Cathedral of the Immaculate Conception are in the upper left. COURTESY ALBANY PUBLIC LIBRARY

RIGHT: Hydorn Blacksmith Shop, Boyntonville, 1910. David Hydorn identified third from left. Also identified in the photo are Wesley Weeden and John Campbell.
COURTESY PITTSTOWN HISTORICAL SOCIETY

LEFT: D. C. Gould store, Clarksville, circa 1910. Gould was married to Mary Blodgett, the adopted daughter of Mr. and Mrs. Adam Clark, for whom Clarksville was named. Along with selling soda and confections, he also repaired clocks and watches out of his store. To the right of the store was the carriage shed and ballroom for the Central Hotel. The hotel and store both burned down in 1912. COURTESY CLARKSVILLE HISTORICAL SOCIETY

OPPOSITE: Rabbler at work at a puddling furnace, Cohoes Rolling Mill, Cohoes, 1911. The mill sat opposite to Star Woolen Mills, on the bank of the Mohawk River. According to an 1869 description, "The mill and auxiliary buildings cover an area of ground measuring 500 by 160 feet. The firm produces shafting, bar and band iron, iron for making gas and steam pipe, trestle work for buildings and bridges, together with a superior quality of axe, pick and mattock poles—the poles being made by means of a patented machine." A fire in 1883 forced the company to rebuild, and the resulting works were capable of producing some 30,000 to 50,000 tons of iron annually. COURTESY NEW YORK STATE ARCHIVES

BELOW LEFT: General Store in Cropseyville, circa 1915. COURTESY BRUNSWICK HISTORICAL SOCIETY

RIGHT: B. T. Babbitt Company building in downtown Albany, owned by Ira Mendleson, circa 1939.
COURTESY STEPHANIE WACHOLDER AND IRA MENDLESON III

BELOW RIGHT: B. T. Babbitt Company owner Ira Mendleson in his office, circa 1925. In 1851, Benjamin Talbot Babbitt started Babbitt's Best Soaps, and quickly became known for his ability to market products. He was the first to market individual bars of soap, the first manufacturer to offer tours of his factories, and also one of the first to give free product samples. After his death, the company passed to his daughters, and later to his grandson Benjamin Talbot Babbitt Hyde. A. Mendleson and Sons, owned by founder Aaron Mendleson's son Ira at the time, bought out several existing soap manufacturers in 1918, including the firm owned by Benjamin Talbot Babbitt Hyde.
COURTESY STEPHANIE WACHOLDER AND IRA MENDLESON III

BELOW: Two young ladies posing on a horse-drawn road grader, Petersburgh, circa 1915. COURTESY TOWN OF PETERSBURGH

ABOVE: Gardeners Grocery Store at 402 Sixteenth Street, Watervliet, circa 1920.
COURTESY WATERVLIET HISTORICAL SOCIETY

ABOVE LEFT: Workers in one of the Coeymans brickyards, circa 1925.
COURTESY HARRY A. STURGES FOR RAVENA COEYMANS HISTORICAL SOCIETY

LEFT: Spillway construction at the Alcove Reservoir in southern Albany County, 1929.
COURTESY HARRY A. STURGES FOR RAVENA COEYMANS HISTORICAL SOCIETY

ABOVE: Photographer Ralph MacDougall demonstrating picture printing to Franciscans from St. Anthony's-on-the-Hudson, who came to *The Knickerbocker News* plant to see what happens to news before it appears in the paper, Rensselaer, April 13, 1938. Fellow Photographer Edward Driscoll snapped the photo in the darkroom. Front row, from left: the Reverend Joel Arnold, the Reverend Bernadine Golden, Friar Lionel Sullivan, Photographer MacDougall. Behind are the Reverend Claude Simson, Friar Basil Corbett, and Friar Emil Drancewicz.
COURTESY TIMES UNION HISTORIC IMAGES

ABOVE RIGHT: Danker Large Tree Moving truck, Albany, 1939.
COURTESY MARILYN STANGLE

OPPOSITE: Niagara Hudson Coke plant in Troy on September 30, 1937. The plant was built in 1924 to manufacture gas by the New York Power and Light Corporation, but was used for several purposes over its lifetime. COURTESY NEW YORK STATE ARCHIVES

RIGHT: Loading lumber and brick on the dock at the Port of Albany, 1932. COURTESY ALBANY PUBLIC LIBRARY

chapter four

MILITARY AND PUBLIC SERVICE

In the digital files of the New York State Archives, you can scroll through the abstracts of some of the notable New Yorkers who served in the conflict known first as the Great War and just a few decades later as World War I. Historians have said that the Empire State contributed more personnel to the war than any other state.

You can click through them: Humphrey Bogart, 18-year-old seaman second class; Russian-born Irving Berlin, demobilized in January 1919 just a few months after writing "God Bless America."

You'll also find the single-card record of the service of Henry Lincoln Johnson, address 23 Monroe Street in Albany, at the foot of Sheridan Hollow.

Johnson—who had worked various jobs, including working as a porter at Union Station just a few blocks from his home—volunteered in June 1917 and enlisted in the all-Black regiment known as the "Harlem Hellfighters." In France's Argonne Forest in May 1918, Johnson fought off a German raid in vicious hand-to-hand combat, and suffered 21 wounds.

For that valor, he became the first American in the war to be awarded the Croix de Guerre.

It took considerably longer for his own country to honor his valor. Despite the volume of his wounds, he didn't receive the Purple Heart until 1996 and the Distinguished Service Cross in 2002. He finally received the Medal of Honor from President Barack Obama in 2015—more than 85 years after his death.

In the following pages, you'll see Capital Region residents who fought often less bloody battles, whether against fire, disease, even tooth decay, or those who demonstrated for a woman's right to vote—the last a battle that wouldn't see national victory until 1920. There are also displays of civic pageantry and mourning befitting the tragedies of the age, from the deaths of presidents to the memorialization of the Civil War.

Casey Seiler

OPPOSITE: Nurses weighing infants in the Ellis Hospital maternity ward in Schenectady, circa 1925. Ellis Hospital was born from the Schenectady Free Dispensary, a five-bed ward located at 408 Union Street and opened on December 25, 1885. Through the support of the community and Charles G. Ellis, president of Schenectady Locomotive Works, the new 30-bed Ellis Hospital was built in 1893.
COURTESY SCHENECTADY COUNTY HISTORICAL SOCIETY, NEW YORK HERITAGE DIGITAL COLLECTIONS

State Street decorated for the funeral of President Lincoln, 1865.
COURTESY ALBANY INSTITUTE OF HISTORY & ART

ABOVE: Army or National Guard encampment at West Sand Lake, July 1895. COURTESY SAND LAKE HISTORICAL SOCIETY

LEFT: J. W. McKnight Hose Company, Village of Castleton-on-Hudson, 1880. An account of the fire department can be found in the 1897 book *Landmarks of Rensselaer County, New York* by George Baker Anderson: "The village has a very efficient fire department, consisting of the Frank P. Harder engine company and the J. W. McKnight hose company. The Frank P. Harder engine company was organized in 1871, it having been found necessary on account of the frequency with which fires occurred. ...About 1,600 feet of hose was also bought and this, with other necessary paraphernalia, comprised the department apparatus... The J. W. McKnight hose company was organized in 1891 and has twenty active members. The original officers were Stephen Cornstock, foreman; Abraham Shortsleeves, first assistant; John Van Buren, secretary; J. W. McKnight, treasurer."
COURTESY VILLAGE OF CASTLETON-ON-HUDSON

ABOVE: Funeral procession for General Ulysses S. Grant at State and Pearl Streets in Albany, 1885. COURTESY ALBANY PUBLIC LIBRARY

ABOVE RIGHT: US Army soldiers in the Watervliet Arsenal standing at attention for an inspection on September 21, 1898. At the time of publication this is the oldest continuously active arsenal in the United States, and produces much of the artillery for the army, as well as gun tubes for cannons, mortars, and tanks. COURTESY WATERVLIET HISTORICAL SOCIETY

RIGHT: Sailors leaving Albany, 1917. COURTESY ALBANY INSTITUTE OF HISTORY & ART

ABOVE: Firefighters of the J. B. Newland Hose Company and E. I. Wood Steamer Company with a Stillwater and Mechanicville Street Railway Company streetcar, 1900. Stillwater's first piece of fire equipment was purchased in 1875. Stillwater No. 1 was a Button Hand Engine, and its purchase signified the creation of the Stillwater Fire Department. In 1886, the department purchased a steam pumper, around the same time that the village purchased the recently vacated Methodist Church building on School Street. The church was renovated, and the steamer was given a home. Two fire companies were formed then as well: The J. B. Newland Hose Company, and the E. I. Wood Steamer Company.
COURTESY STILLWATER PUBLIC LIBRARY AND THE HISTORIAN'S OFFICE

ABOVE LEFT: A march for women's suffrage led by the Socialist party in Schenectady, 1912. COURTESY ALBANY INSTITUTE OF HISTORY & ART

LEFT: Stillwater Post Office, early 1900s. Postmaster Frank Stump identified at far right.
COURTESY STILLWATER PUBLIC LIBRARY AND THE HISTORIAN'S OFFICE

RIGHT: A march for women's suffrage led by Socialists in Schenectady, 1912. COURTESY ALBANY INSTITUTE OF HISTORY & ART

OPPOSITE: Civic Improvement work crew planting an elm tree on one of the principal streets in Albany, April 26, 1915. COURTESY NEW YORK STATE ARCHIVES

BELOW RIGHT: Prominent suffragists in Albany, circa 1912. Identified in the photo: Miss E. Brannan, Miss J. Schneiderman, Mrs. M. S. Smith, Mrs. John Rogers, Miss E. Mayer. COURTESY ALBANY INSTITUTE OF HISTORY & ART

BELOW: Attendants in the Assembly document room in the New York State Capitol, March 1914. COURTESY NEW YORK STATE ARCHIVES

ABOVE: World War I Lieutenant Elmer White, South Glens Falls, Moreau, circa 1917. COURTESY PARKS-BENTLEY PLACE, HISTORICAL SOCIETY OF MOREAU AND SOUTH GLENS FALLS

LEFT: Henry Perrault, Cohoes, circa 1917. COURTESY HOGAN FAMILY ARCHIVES

OPPOSITE: Sunday afternoon tea for soldiers of the US Army Watervliet Arsenal, hosted in the YMCA in Troy, circa 1917. COURTESY NEW YORK STATE ARCHIVES

ABOVE: US Army Watervliet Arsenal Fire Department in 1918. The department responded to many fires in the area.
COURTESY WATERVLIET HISTORICAL SOCIETY

ABOVE RIGHT: Honor Guard on lower State Street escorting bodies of Albany soldiers killed in action in World War I, circa 1917. COURTESY ALBANY PUBLIC LIBRARY

OPPOSITE TOP LEFT: Women of the American Red Cross auxiliary standing on and around the tank Britannia in Albany, March 12, 1918. COURTESY NEW YORK STATE ARCHIVES

OPPOSITE TOP RIGHT: War Chest Parade at State and Eagle Streets in Albany, 1916. COURTESY ALBANY PUBLIC LIBRARY

OPPOSITE BOTTOM: Soldiers in formation near a sports field at the Rensselaer Polytechnic Institute campus in Troy, circa 1917. The Rensselaer School was established in 1824 by Stephen Van Rensselaer. The goal of the school, in his own words, was "for the purpose of instructing persons ... in the application of science to the common purposes of life." The name was changed to the Rensselaer Polytechnic Institute in 1861, and the school holds that title at the time of publication.
COURTESY NEW YORK STATE ARCHIVES

RIGHT: The last group of men drafted into service from the Village of Castleton-on-Hudson during World War I, 1918. Identified in the front row: Charles Cook, William Leonard, Julius Heinger. Second row: Frank McCluskey, Frank Faw, Harry Snyder. Back row: Fred Broden, Ed Barton, Ralph Lansing, Clarence Christiansen. COURTESY VILLAGE OF CASTLETON-ON-HUDSON

ABOVE: Police officer in Albany, circa 1920. Room tentatively identified as a New York State Conservation Commission office in Albany's Telephone Building. COURTESY NEW YORK STATE ARCHIVES

ABOVE RIGHT: World War I veterans on the steps of the Reformed Church in Nassau Village on July 4, 1919. The day served both as a 100th anniversary celebration of the village's incorporation, and a welcome home for returning veterans. Events included a service of thanks at the church, a parade, field day at the fairgrounds, and fireworks at dusk. COURTESY VILLAGE OF NASSAU

OPPOSITE: Stenographic room in the Division of Lands and Forests of the New York State Conservation Commission, located in Albany's Telephone Building, 1920. Employees, from left: May B. Grimes, N. S. Slocum, Rosine Mullarkey. COURTESY NEW YORK STATE ARCHIVES

RIGHT: Selkirk Fire Department, 1931. COURTESY BETHLEHEM HISTORICAL ASSOCIATION

ABOVE: Police officer Karl J. Peters operating the traffic signal at State and Center Streets, Schenectady, 1924.
COURTESY SCHENECTADY COUNTY HISTORICAL SOCIETY

ABOVE LEFT: Engine House No. 1 at Western and Washington Avenues in Albany, March 30, 1920. COURTESY ALBANY INSTITUTE OF HISTORY & ART

OPPOSITE: Nassau Hose Company No. 1 with a newly purchased American LaFrance fire engine, 1926. The company was founded after a devastating fire in 1901. COURTESY VILLAGE OF NASSAU

LEFT: Selkirk Fire Department trucks parked outside Lehmann's Garage in Selkirk, circa 1930. COURTESY BETHLEHEM HISTORICAL ASSOCIATION

New York Governor Franklin Delano Roosevelt in front of the park headquarters at Saratoga Battlefield, circa 1929. During his tenure as governor of New York, which lasted until he was elected President in 1932, Roosevelt would give guided tours of the battlefield to foreign dignitaries. After becoming president he pushed to have the field made a National Park. COURTESY NEW YORK STATE ARCHIVES

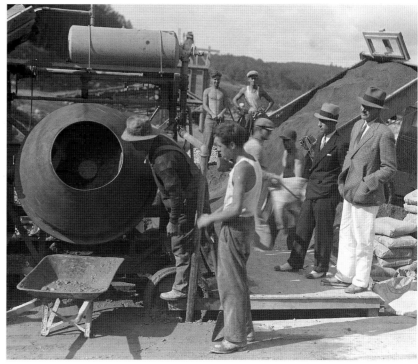

ABOVE: Construction work at the Cherry Plain wildlife refuge (later became the Capital District State Wildlife Management Area, which includes Cherry Plain State Park) by members of the Civilian Conservation Corps near Cherry Plain in Berlin, circa 1936. New York State Conservation Commissioner Lithgow Osborne (in office 1933–1938) can be seen first from the right. COURTESY NEW YORK STATE ARCHIVES

ABOVE LEFT: Troy City Mission, 191 River Street, circa 1930. COURTESY ALBANY INSTITUTE OF HISTORY & ART

LEFT: A student having his teeth fixed up in St. Peter's outpatient department, Albany, October 13, 1935. During the previous year 5,039 school children were referred to the free clinics of the three general hospitals for treatment. Of this number 1,113 were dental cases. COURTESY TIMES UNION HISTORIC IMAGES

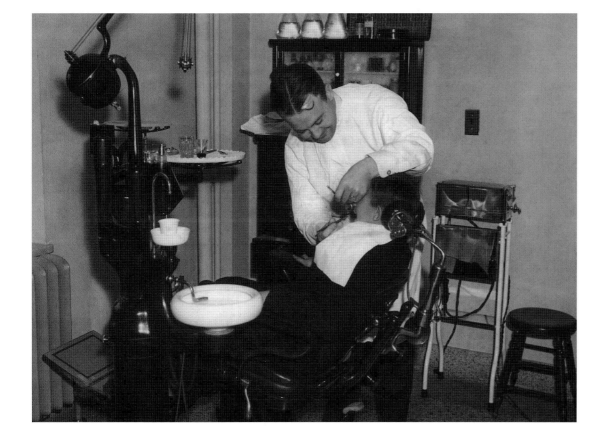

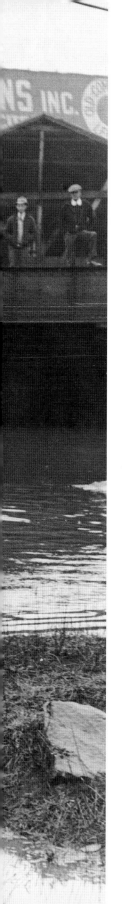

chapter five

DISASTERS

Nature still overwhelms us, just not as often as in the past. Surveying the images in this chapter, the latest from 1938, what's most remarkable is how familiar the toll from elemental carnage can seem. Most of the havoc is caused by water, in multiple forms, in large part related to the Capital Region being at the confluence of two rivers.

Locks and other engineering efforts notwithstanding, the Mohawk River continues to swamp part of Schenectady's historic Stockade district almost every year. As recently as 2011, it also engulfed much of Rotterdam Junction, located 8 miles upstream. The Atlantic Ocean's tidal influence on the Hudson River, combined with the inflow from the Mohawk, can still make a mess of things. It happened in 1938, when an unnamed hurricane devastated Long Island and southern New England and made the Hudson temporarily impassable for ships trying to leave the Port of Albany. It happened again in 2011, when remnants of Hurricane Irene wrought terrible destruction to the Mohawk Valley.

Water's colder incarnations, snow and ice, bring their own woes. The Albany area gets about 5 feet of snow per cold season. (Syracuse averages literally twice as much, so we really shouldn't complain.) Sometimes it's much worse: In the winter of 1887-88, a whopper of a blizzard dumped New York's capital city with 110 inches. (In 1970–71, another storm dropped 112 inches.) Modern machinery makes us much better at getting rid of it—take a look at page 84 for a look at how the community had to come together with shovels alongside the state Capitol after the Blizzard of 1888. But even today, snow still calms and quiets life, if only for a while.

Our response to disaster seems most improved in the areas of fire and major transportation accidents. A century ago, train crashes were almost commonplace, with one route alone, the Albany-Hudson Fast Line, recording multiple serious crashes and derailments during its operation in the years around the turn of the 20th century. Fires remain a sad fact of contemporary life. But deaths from structure fires fall every year, locally and nationwide. The number of lives lost to fires dropped by an average of 50 percent across America from 1977 to 2017, for example, and, thankfully, the killer conflagrations of the past—including the same night in October 1871, when the Great Chicago Fire claimed 300 lives and 18,000 buildings, and 1,200 died by fire 250 miles north in Peshtigo, Wisconsin—seem likely never to be repeated.

No matter the cause and regardless of the year, disasters pull communities together, in grief and in resolve, and in our collective response we find our collective humanity.

Steve Barnes

OPPOSITE: Navigating floodwaters on Weaver Street in Schenectady, March 12, 1936. Efforts of the State Canal employees to keep the ice and water flowing using dynamite had proven futile in the face of continued rain and snow. The flood, which began on the 12th, would reach its peak one week later at 17.5 inches above normal river flow. COURTESY SCHENECTADY COUNTY HISTORICAL SOCIETY, NEW YORK HERITAGE DIGITAL COLLECTIONS

ABOVE: Snow piled high in front of a furnishing goods store at 27 North Pearl Street in Albany after the Blizzard of 1888. Identified in the photo are James W. Kearney, Edwin Palmer, and Minnie B. Kearney. Albany County Bank, erected in 1887, can be seen at far right.
COURTESY ALBANY INSTITUTE OF HISTORY & ART

ABOVE RIGHT: Nassau residents overlooking the aftermath of the fire that destroyed the Van Valkenburgh Hotel, 1890. Notable guests of the hotel included the Marquis de Lafayette, Joseph Bonaparte, and President Martin Van Buren. COURTESY VILLAGE OF NASSAU

RIGHT: Looking west up Washington Avenue from Albany City Hall as people dig out after the Blizzard of 1888. Although the city had survived just over 2.5 feet of snow three months prior, the bulk of that snow all fell in a day—the largest single-day snowfall in Albany recorded history. On Sunday, March 11, the "Great White Hurricane" overtook Albany and held it at a standstill for the next four days.
COURTESY ALBANY PUBLIC LIBRARY

ABOVE: Schenectady during the Spring Flood of 1893. The road they are standing on is tentatively identified as Washington Avenue. While flooding in the spring due to ice jams and rain was not unique, this flood was atypical in that the jams forced the flood waters into the Erie Canal thereby flooding the south portion of Schenectady. Areas normally flooded, such as Frog Alley and Rotterdam Street, were left relatively unharmed, while Kruesi Avenue, Delaware Avenue, and Delaware Street were under six feet of water. Losses were estimated to be as high as $100,000.
COURTESY SCHENECTADY COUNTY HISTORICAL SOCIETY, NEW YORK HERITAGE DIGITAL COLLECTIONS

LEFT: A Fitchburg Railroad train that tumbled into the Hoosic River on October 5, 1889. Torrential rains and flooding had washed out the tracks in several places along the line between Eagle Bridge and Hoosick Junction.
COURTESY HOOSICK TOWNSHIP HISTORICAL SOCIETY

ABOVE: Church and Elm Streets under water after a flood devastated much of downtown Hoosick Falls, October 5, 1898. COURTESY HOOSICK TOWNSHIP HISTORICAL SOCIETY

OPPOSITE: Damage to barges and Erie Canal structure due to a canal blowout a mile and a half above the hamlet of Pattersonville in Rotterdam, 1895.
COURTESY SCHENECTADY COUNTY HISTORICAL SOCIETY, NEW YORK HERITAGE DIGITAL COLLECTIONS

ABOVE: Albany City Hall, designed by Philip Hooker, after being destroyed by fire on February 10, 1880. COURTESY ALBANY PUBLIC LIBRARY

ABOVE RIGHT: Navigating the floodwaters cutting off the Schenectady Boat Club, March 1, 1910. Rising temperatures and heavy rains met with an ice jam near Crescent on February 27, leading to the second significant flood of the century. From the *Schenectady Gazette*, February 28, 1910, "a new high flood record was established, when at 1 o'clock this morning the Mohawk River had overflowed its bounds and inundated a considerable portion of the lower part of the city. The flooded area was even greater than in the fall of 1903, when the city experienced the most disastrous inundation in its history."
COURTESY SCHENECTADY COUNTY HISTORICAL SOCIETY, NEW YORK HERITAGE DIGITAL COLLECTIONS

RIGHT: Children on a bridge at Fifth Street and Third Avenue as floodwaters from Dry River rush underneath, February 28, 1910. While generally dry, the river was capable of considerable flooding during the spring thaw, or a heavy rain. The Dry River System was constructed in 1912 as a way to control the flooding of the city. A large dam would store the water from a storm, and release it slowly through a system under the streets to the Hudson River. COURTESY WATERVLIET HISTORICAL SOCIETY

Floodwaters at the start of Front Street to the Nott Street Bridge over the Erie Canal, Schenectady, circa 1910.

ABOVE: Looking east from James Street to Maiden Lane and Broadway on March 28 in Albany, during the Great Flood of 1913. Business on the left is B. Payne and Sons Tobacco Company. COURTESY ALBANY INSTITUTE OF HISTORY & ART

ABOVE LEFT: State Library Reading Room after the Capital Fire, Albany, March 29, 1911. The Capitol Building was constructed over 32 years, between 1867 and 1899. The library and much of its collections were destroyed in only a few hours. Visible in the upper left are the remains of a circular frame from the burned-out clock. Remarkably, manuscript records of the War of 1812 were found intact in a closet next to the clock. COURTESY ALBANY INSTITUTE OF HISTORY & ART

OPPOSITE: Mohawk River flooding in Schenectady, circa 1913. COURTESY SCHENECTADY COUNTY HISTORICAL SOCIETY, NEW YORK HERITAGE DIGITAL COLLECTIONS

LEFT: Sixteenth Street looking east during the flood of 1913. When rivers in the central and eastern United States became swollen from runoff and heavy rains, flooding occurred that would take the lives of approximately 650 people and leave a quarter million people homeless. Due to its severity, many expected this was a 100-year flood. History was due to repeat itself much sooner however, when heavy snow melts once again caused major flooding exactly one year later. COURTESY WATERVLIET HISTORICAL SOCIETY

LEFT: A surprisingly jovial man helping a friend use a overturned side table as a boat at 369 Broadway in Schenectady, 1914.
COURTESY SCHENECTADY COUNTY HISTORICAL SOCIETY, NEW YORK HERITAGE DIGITAL COLLECTIONS

OPPOSITE TOP RIGHT: Looking east from Broadway at State Street in Schenectady after the blizzard of February 13 and 14, 1914. The storm left 32 inches of snow in the city, on top of the snow and ice already there from the especially cold winter. An abrupt rise in temperature soon brought heavy, warm rains to the Mohawk Valley, and on March 27 the ice and water in the Schoharie Creek broke free and smashed into the Mohawk River.
COURTESY SCHENECTADY COUNTY HISTORICAL SOCIETY, NEW YORK HERITAGE DIGITAL COLLECTIONS

OPPOSITE TOP LEFT: Horse-drawn carts trying to make their way on Dock Street during a flood in Schenectady, March 28, 1914. Caused by an ice jam breaking free after freezing temperatures gave way to warm rains on the previous day, a deluge tore through the Mohawk Valley, destroying the majority of bridges as it went. In Schenectady it flooded shops and swept away residents, only some of whom were found alive, clinging to debris down river. The peak of the flood on March 28 set a record high water line of 232.9 feet at the Mohawk River, the mark from which can still be seen at the time of publication.
COURTESY SCHENECTADY COUNTY HISTORICAL SOCIETY, NEW YORK HERITAGE DIGITAL COLLECTIONS

OPPOSITE BOTTOM: Navigating floodwaters on Front Street in Schenectady, March 28, 1914.
COURTESY SCHENECTADY COUNTY HISTORICAL SOCIETY, NEW YORK HERITAGE DIGITAL COLLECTIONS

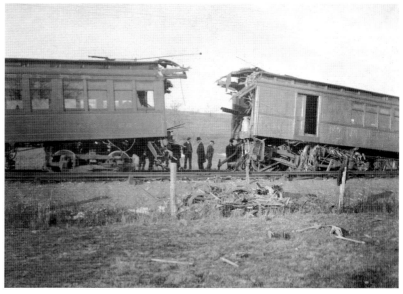

ABOVE: Two railcars split apart after a crash on the Albany-Hudson Fast Line, south of Nassau Village near Sweet's Crossing, September 24, 1905. Rail service on the Albany-Hudson Fast Line offered both passenger and freight service. Over the 29-year run of the service, several serious accidents took place. Cars could reach a top speed of about 60 miles per hour. COURTESY VILLAGE OF NASSAU

ABOVE LEFT: John Street in Hoosick Falls after a fire wiped out the Easton Thorpe and Lurie blocks on March 20, 1915. An article from the *Syracuse Herald* on the 21st described the damage done to the town, "Fire, which started in the Easton Thorpe block, presumably from a heater, and spread to four business blocks, burned one residence and now threatens the entire business section of the town. Calls for help have been sent to fire departments in Troy, North Adams, Bennington and Cambridge. No loss of life is reported. Within an hour the loss amounted to between $100,000 and $200,000." COURTESY HOOSICK TOWNSHIP HISTORICAL SOCIETY

OPPOSITE: The Church Street side of the Easton Thorpe block in Hoosick Falls after a fire devastated downtown on March 20, 1915. The fire started in the basement of the Thorpe building and rapidly spread to adjacent structures.
COURTESY HOOSICK TOWNSHIP HISTORICAL SOCIETY

LEFT: Train wreck at Schodack, 1918.
COURTESY VILLAGE OF CASTLETON-ON-HUDSON

ABOVE: Blizzard in Clarksville, March 27, 1932.
COURTESY CLARKSVILLE HISTORICAL SOCIETY

ABOVE RIGHT: Aftermath in Clarksville after the Great Fire of August 22, 1918. According to the *Altamont Enterprise* of August 30, 1918: "It is estimated that no less than 1,500 automobiles visited the ruins of the fire here on Sunday. Each car was filled so that perhaps 10,000 people were here on that day, and ever since the fire last Thursday, the village has been filled with cars, coming and going, to witness the terrible destruction caused by the flames."
COURTESY CLARKSVILLE HISTORICAL SOCIETY

RIGHT: Tour ship *Alexander Hamilton* of the Hudson River Day Line is unable to sail out of Albany because of high water following a hurricane, September 22, 1938. COURTESY TIMES UNION HISTORIC IMAGES

Cars sinking into the mire of Quackenkill Creek, at intersection of South Road and Route 2 in Brunswick, after a hurricane in the fall of 1938. The storm had formed on the coast of Africa on September 9, becoming a Category 5 hurricane before moving toward the east coast of the United States and making landfall on September 21 as a Category 3. It altered the shoreline of Long Island, washed away bridges, severed train service between New York and Boston, and also brought down 20,000 miles of power and telephone lines. While flooding and damage did occur in the Capital Region, one indicator of how comparatively lucky the area was during this storm is the highest reported wind velocity in Albany of 42 miles per hour. This paled in comparison with wind speeds well over 100 miles per hour in other cities.

COURTESY BRUNSWICK HISTORICAL SOCIETY

chapter six

EDUCATION

ope and optimism about the future are implicit in education. The first university as we would recognize it was founded in 1088, in Bologna, Italy; the first American public school, Boston Latin, began instruction in 1635, only 15 years after the ship the Mayflower brought Pilgrims to what would become known as New England. The oldest independent school for girls in the United States, the Albany Academy for Girls, launched in 1814 as the Albany Female Academy, predating the city's public school system by a decade and a half. As recently as the beginning of the 21st century, a newer educational model, charter schools, started to blossom in the capital city.

Informing all is the belief that the multidisciplinary instruction of future generations is essential to improving society. The city of Schenectady's system, founded in 1854, has 17 buildings and 9,200 pupils in kindergarten through 12th grade; the suburban Shenendehowa district, in southern Saratoga County, draws 9,800 enrollees from an 86 square mile area; the 10,000 students of Albany's public school cost $234 million a year to educate.

Looking through the six decades of photos in this chapter we see elements common to today—science and language, sports and the arts—and, indeed, to the ancient Greece of 25 centuries ago, when a "gumnastike" curriculum trained the body while its "mousike" counterpart stressed the humanities. What's shockingly unlike today is the racial homogeneity: Of the 30 photos in this chapter, among all the faculty, students and staff shown, there appears to be a single nonwhite person: In a 1910 photo from Albany Public School No. 7, there are 33 students, who look to be in their early elementary years. On one side, so far at the edge of the photo that part of her is cropped from the image, is a girl with dark skin. Today in the city school district, white students represent about the same percentage, one-fifth, as their Hispanic and Asian counterparts, with Black students at nearly half the population.

Faces and instructional particulars change; the mission does not. Take a look at a band photo from page 112, of the Castleton-on-Hudson senior band: five boys, three girls, a female band director. Maybe clothing, and the presence of two banjos among eight players total, gives away the period. But these kids look like they can swing.

Steve Barnes

OPPOSITE: Children playing on the slide in the Schenectady School's playground, circa 1910. COURTESY NEW YORK STATE ARCHIVES

RIGHT: The student body of District 3 Union Free School on Mountain Road, Ravena, circa 1890s.
COURTESY HARRY A. STURGES FOR RAVENA COEYMANS HISTORICAL SOCIETY

OPPOSITE: Students from the New York State Normal College at Albany class of 1897. There were many changes to the school over the years, a number of which were related to its name. A brief history of the school can be found on their website, "In 1844, a 'normal school' was founded in Albany to train teachers for a rapidly growing population. For nearly 50 years, the Normal School provided a two-year education to students from across the state. By 1890, the evolving school system in New York required a new approach to teacher training. The Normal School gradually made changes: a four-year program, new curricula, new faculty, and new standards for student enrollment. In 1914, the institution officially became known as the New York State College for Teachers..." In 1959 the name was changed to State University of New York College of Education at Albany, in 1961 to State University of New York College at Albany, and in 1962 to State University of New York at Albany. The current name has been in place since 1986, University at Albany, SUNY.
COURTESY M.E. GRENANDER DEPARTMENT OF SPECIAL COLLECTIONS & ARCHIVES, UNIVERSITY AT ALBANY, SUNY

BELOW RIGHT: Students and teacher outside Stephentown school, circa 1890. COURTESY HART CLUETT MUSEUM

BELOW: Students from the New York State Normal School class of 1880 on the steps of the school's Lodge Street Building, Albany.
COURTESY M.E. GRENANDER DEPARTMENT OF SPECIAL COLLECTIONS & ARCHIVES, UNIVERSITY AT ALBANY, SUNY

ABOVE: Schenectady High School students at the bus stop, circa 1905. COURTESY SCHENECTADY COUNTY HISTORICAL SOCIETY

ABOVE LEFT: Students at Millertown School on Herrington Road, Pittstown, early 1900s. Included in photo: Mary Rose, Madeline Griffin, Emily Herrington, Maud Warnen, Mary Cottrell, Mary Ryan, Ethel Morse, Teacher, Grace Marshall, Harry Brundige, Chester Warren, Lottie Warren, Walter Marshall, Edgar Cottrell, Howard Herrington, Abraham Herrington, Cornelius Ryan, Gerard Ryan, Sherman Herrington. COURTESY PITTSTOWN HISTORICAL SOCIETY

BELOW LEFT: Students and teacher at Cropseyville School in Brunswick, 1898. COURTESY BRUNSWICK HISTORICAL SOCIETY

Ravena High School baseball team, 1907. COURTESY HARRY A. STURGES FOR RAVENA COEYMANS HISTORICAL SOCIETY

Folk dancing, Schenectady City Schools, circa 1910. COURTESY NEW YORK STATE ARCHIVES

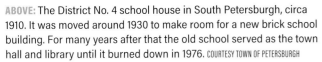

ABOVE: The District No. 4 school house in South Petersburgh, circa 1910. It was moved around 1930 to make room for a new brick school building. For many years after that the old school served as the town hall and library until it burned down in 1976. COURTESY TOWN OF PETERSBURGH

ABOVE RIGHT: Little Red Schoolhouse, in the North Greenbush Common School District, 1907. COURTESY GREENBUSH HISTORICAL SOCIETY

RIGHT: Sacred Heart Parochial School, Village of Castleton-on-Hudson, 1906. COURTESY VILLAGE OF CASTLETON-ON-HUDSON

ABOVE: Public School No. 7, on Clinton Avenue just west of Swan Street, Albany, circa 1910. This school building still stands at the time of publication. COURTESY ALBANY PUBLIC LIBRARY

ABOVE LEFT: Bloomingrove School in North Greenbush, circa 1910.
COURTESY GREENBUSH HISTORICAL SOCIETY

LEFT: Elmer Avenue School in Schenectady, circa 1911. COURTESY SCHENECTADY COUNTY HISTORICAL SOCIETY

ABOVE: Model High School at New York State Normal College at Albany, under the direction of principal John M. Sayles, class of 1910. Identified students: Mary Gauger, Maleska Spears, Rachel Griswold, Jessie Luck, Ruth Thompson, Iona Pier, Marguerite Butler, Sadie Moran, Mary Walsh, Edna Moat, Walter Hurst, Raymond Lindsay, Warren Vosburg, Joseph Broderick, George Anderson, Mr. Morton, Charles Grounds, Harold Goewey. In 1914, Model High School was renamed Milne School, and New York State Normal College became New York State College for Teachers at Albany. It would eventually become State University of New York at Albany. Principal Sayles went on to become the director of teacher training at the college from 1920–1939, acting president from 1939–1943, and president from 1943–1947. COURTESY ALBANY PUBLIC LIBRARY

OPPOSITE: Mary Mathers' class at School 10 in Bemis Heights, fall 1914. COURTESY STILLWATER PUBLIC LIBRARY AND THE HISTORIAN'S OFFICE

RIGHT: Albany Business College at 83–87 North Pearl Street at Columbia Street, Albany, circa 1925. This building still stands at the time of publication. COURTESY ALBANY PUBLIC LIBRARY

ABOVE: Students in costume for a play at Elmer Avenue School in Schenectady, circa 1920.
COURTESY SCHENECTADY COUNTY HISTORICAL SOCIETY

RIGHT: Students making oakum pads under the direction of the Chairman of the Surgical Dressings Committee at Vocational School in Troy in the fall of 1917. Oakum is a loose fiber made by untwisting old rope and soaking in tar to reduce it to its original material. It became popular in the medical field because it was inexpensive, absorbent, soft, and the smell of the tar would reduce foul odors. COURTESY NEW YORK STATE ARCHIVES

LEFT: Schenectady High School Interscholastic Cross County Run champions, 1923. COURTESY SCHENECTADY COUNTY HISTORICAL SOCIETY

BELOW LEFT: South Glens Falls area high school play, class of 1922. From left: Florence Bennett, Clifton Sipley, George Palmer, Ruth Freebern, Dorian Blackbird, Marion Greenewood, Wilson Clark (dressed as a girl), Thelma Freeman, Arthur LaVoy. COURTESY PARKS-BENTLEY PLACE, HISTORICAL SOCIETY OF MOREAU AND SOUTH GLENS FALLS

BELOW: Eighth-grade graduation at School 15 in Albany, 1924. COURTESY JACK GHEZZI

ABOVE: South High girl's basketball team, 1927-1931. From left: Margaret Hay, Gladys Dixon, Ora Wood, Rocky Williams, Doris Noonan, Jean Godetta, Edith Colby, Sis Greenwood. COURTESY PARKS-BENTLEY PLACE, HISTORICAL SOCIETY OF MOREAU AND SOUTH GLENS FALLS

ABOVE LEFT: Second graders at Nassau Elementary School shortly after the new school was built in 1939. Previously up to 14 one-room schoolhouses served the town; by 1939, all area children were educated in the same building. COURTESY VILLAGE OF NASSAU

OPPOSITE: Senior orchestra, Village of Castleton-on-Hudson, February 1927. Seated, from left: Edward Roland, Cornelia Vanderplas, Herbert Speiska, Kellie (Richtor) Nichols. Standing: Malcom Metzger, Sheldyn Leonard, Elsworth Chapman, Florence Haber, Director Richards. COURTESY VILLAGE OF CASTLETON-ON-HUDSON

LEFT: Emma Willard's Temple of Time being exhibited at Emma Willard School's 125th anniversary celebration at Troy, October 6, 1939. The exhibit is being inspected by, from left: Betsy Dibert, of Troy; Katharine Schacht, of Troy; Virginia Holmes, of Troy; Mary Polk, of Troy; and Louise Hubbell, of Loudonville. COURTESY TIMES UNION HISTORIC IMAGES

chapter seven

COMMUNITY

Even in today's divided and diverse times, you can still see examples of community in the Capital Region. In one local city, it might be a bumper sticker that suggests you "Enjoy Troy" or a T-shirt that announces "South Troy Against the World."

But "community," that sense of belonging and fellowship, has long been ingrained in the area. You can find it in the surviving remnants of Dutch culture, culminating in Albany's yearly Tulip Fest and Pinksterfest, complete with clogged and costumed young women scrubbing the streets in traditional fashion. It's evident in the numerous community centers, gathering proud Italians, Poles, Irish, Russians, Chinese, and other nationalities together to celebrate their heritages.

Predominately Black neighborhoods like Arbor Hill in Albany and Hamilton Hill in Schenectady have long worked to forge their own identities, honoring and acknowledging their pasts while forging positive paths to the future. You see it in the increased awareness and influence of the Juneteenth holiday and the long struggle to get local World War I hero Henry Johnson his proper due.

Religion has always been integral to the Capital Region. The spires and stonework of centuries-old churches still dot the landscape, alongside temples, mosques, and meeting places. Over the years, they've been joined by Buddhist temples, Hindu temples, and peace pagodas. The famed Shaker Heritage Society still exists, even as it shares space with the Albany International Airport.

Travel among the cities and towns of the area and you'll find communities within communities, carried down from generation to generation. Boy Scouts and Girls Scouts, 4-H clubs, military veterans, Elks, Knights of Columbus, women's groups, men's groups, and far too many more to mention.

Arts and culture, alternative or mainstream, have also had their own sense of community, whether centrally located in pockets of activity, or spread out across the region. Lark Street in Albany, the Beekman Street Arts District in Saratoga Springs, Woodstock, and Hudson are just a few examples of local arts scenes.

And charity may begin, but never stays, at home. The number of groups and organizations that have done and are doing charitable work in the Capital Region, and the causes they have served, is impressive, and can bring people together in ways nothing else can—including orphaned and poor children, older residents, mental health patients, people suffering from diseases and their families, the environment, historical landmarks, schools, churches, and many more.

C.J. Lais

....

OPPOSITE: Troy Orphan Asylum boys picking currants for the Red Cross at Clapp Farm, Kinderhook, in July 1917. The forerunner to the asylum was the Benevolent Society of Troy to Assist Indigent Women and Children, started in 1800. With a vision of caring for orphaned children, the Society opened the Troy Orphan Asylum in 1833, and it was soon incorporated by the State of New York. In 1942 the name of the building was changed to Vanderheyden Hall to reflect the ideals of Troy's founders, the Van Der Heyden family. By 2014 they had expanded to providing housing and services throughout the Capital Region, and so the "Hall" was dropped. At the time of publication they are still serving the community, providing "safe haven for children, youth and adults who have experienced family disruption, emotional difficulty and learning problems." COURTESY NEW YORK STATE ARCHIVES

ABOVE: Member of the Vosburgh family, identified as either Rosennah or Anna Vosburgh, Albany, December 22, 1871. COURTESY ALBANY INSTITUTE OF HISTORY & ART

ABOVE RIGHT: Gardens of the Walter A. Wood estate in Hoosick Township, circa 1878. Built in 1873 and modeled after an English castle, the Wood mansion overlooked Main Street. After the closing of the Wood plant, the mansion was given to the Village of Hoosick Falls to become the high school. It was demolished in 1969, and the entrance to the estate became Wood Memorial Park. COURTESY HOOSICK TOWNSHIP HISTORICAL SOCIETY

RIGHT: Laying the cornerstone of the Jermain Church in Port Schuyler, Watervliet, 1874. COURTESY WATERVLIET HISTORICAL SOCIETY

Mr. and Mrs. Charles Elkenburgh in Grafton, circa 1890. Elkenburgh was a cigar maker at 18 King Street in Troy.
COURTESY GRAFTON HISTORICAL SOCIETY

RIGHT: Myra Bornt (Simmons) using a washing machine when she was about sixteen, Cropseyville, late 1800s. The machine had no electricity as the only gas in the county at the time was in Troy. COURTESY BRUNSWICK HISTORICAL SOCIETY

BELOW: Haying in Grafton, circa 1895. Haying was one of the industries upon which the farmer depended for cash. Tons of hay were taken to the cities for bedding for the many horses, and many more tons were made into bales at the hay presses in the river towns to be shipped to New York. Rye straw was used as insulation in the ice houses found in every town, hamlet, and on most farms. This scene was captured by photographer Elmer Jacobs. COURTESY HART CLUETT MUSEUM

LEFT: The Palmer and Roye families, grist mill operators in Nassau, 1899. Joseph Roye (second from left) was married to Jane Ann Palmer (third from right). The founding of Nassau in the 1700s was based on access to water power and the mills that water could power. COURTESY VILLAGE OF NASSAU

BELOW FAR LEFT: Van Rensselaer family, circa 1890.
COURTESY HISTORIC CHERRY HILL

BELOW LEFT: The Tilting Tennent building on Railroad Street near State Street in Schenectady, circa 1900. The building was later condemned and razed.
COURTESY SCHENECTADY COUNTY HISTORICAL SOCIETY, NEW YORK HERITAGE DIGITAL COLLECTIONS

ABOVE: Evaline Vroman and Orville Deitz, possibly on their wedding day in Cedar Hill, Bethlehem, 1902.
COURTESY SUMMER DEITZ WILBER

LEFT: Smith Abbott feeding his pigs, Baum Road in Pittstown, circa 1905. COURTESY PITTSTOWN HISTORICAL SOCIETY

OPPOSITE: Joseph Allen family along banks of the Poestenkill Creek, circa 1900. COURTESY BRUNSWICK HISTORICAL SOCIETY

RIGHT: Ed Conde family posed on the porch of their house on Upper Wolf Hollow Road, Glenville, 1905. COURTESY GLENVILLE HISTORY CENTER

OPPOSITE TOP LEFT: Barn raising at the Charles Bolander Farm on Longwoods Road, Johnsonville, early 1900s. COURTESY PITTSTOWN HISTORICAL SOCIETY

OPPOSITE TOP RIGHT: Children at Fresh Air Home in Grafton, circa 1914. The home was made possible by the vision of William Anderson, a traveling salesman for the *Troy Times* whose time around the Adirondacks gave him a deep love for the area. He and *Troy Times* owner Charles Spencer Francis created the *Troy Times* Fresh Air Fund to secure funding for city children to board at farms in Rensselaer County. In 1909 the organization had expanded enough that funds could be allocated to purchase property in the mountains in Grafton, and the Fresh Air Home was built. The Fresh Air program continued until 1948. COURTESY GRAFTON HISTORICAL SOCIETY

OPPOSITE BOTTOM: Young women in patriotic costume during World War I, Troy, circa 1918. COURTESY NEW YORK STATE ARCHIVES

BELOW RIGHT: Frederick H. Vogel with his twin Catherine Vogel in Albany, 1912. COURTESY FRITZ VOGEL

BELOW: West Glenville Odd Fellows, 1910. COURTESY GLENVILLE HISTORY CENTER

RIGHT: Gladys Saddlemeyer and her Jersey cow in Knox, 1923. COURTESY NEW YORK STATE ARCHIVES

OPPOSITE: Members of a 4-H Club at East Schodack receiving trees for planting, circa 1925. This image was created to record the reforestation activities of the New York State Conservation Commission or Conservation Department. COURTESY NEW YORK STATE ARCHIVES

BELOW RIGHT: Troy Orphan Asylum girls showing off their pickling skills at the Eastern States Expo in September 1921. The previous year three boys from the Troy Orphan Asylum won second prize. COURTESY VANDERHEYDEN

BELOW: Elizabeth White Allen in Crescent Park, Schenectady, 1917. COURTESY WENDY ALLEN

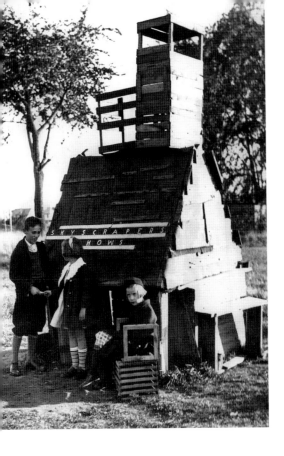

ABOVE: Harvey Holmes (left) selling a ticket for miniature movie show house Skyscrapers Shows to Doris Detiere, while Doris Loucks waits for her turn, Albany, October 15, 1935. The show house was built by neighborhood kids in a vacant lot behind the home of Harvey Holmes. He and Holmes Hecker charged a penny for a ticket to view one cartoon. COURTESY TIMES UNION HISTORIC IMAGES

ABOVE RIGHT: County 4-H Leaders Picnic, West Glenville, circa 1935. Catherine Van der Veer, Sarah Ann Van der Veer, and Jane Van der Veer are included. COURTESY GLENVILLE HISTORY CENTER

RIGHT: Constance "Helen" Bumbarbardatore (left) and Dorothy Mazzarella of Schenectady County in front of the Vose House Nurses Home in Boston, late 1930s. COURTESY MAZZARELLA FAMILY

LEFT: Troy Orphan Asylum Boy Scout troop at Camp Rotary Twin Lakes in Averill Park, 1939. The first uniformed Boy Scout Troop was organized at the Troy Orphan Asylum in 1911. COURTESY VANDERHEYDEN

BELOW LEFT: Schultz Farm on Watervliet Shaker Road, adjacent to the site of the future Albany Airport, 1937. Front row, from left: Margaret Schultz, Bertha (Schultz) Masade, Mildred (Schultz) Selig, Marguerite Schultz, Anna (Wertman) Schultz, Mrs. Ellrott, Marie Schultz, Rose Marie Schultz (infant). Back row: Louis Schultz, Fritz Selig, Warren Schultz, Larry Ellrott, Andy Ellrott, Ray Schultz. COURTESY MARIANNE SCHULTZ

BELOW: Teresa Smith on a traveling photographer's pony with her older sister, Josephine Kennedy, Troy, 1936. COURTESY DEBORAH SMITH

chapter eight

RECREATION AND CELEBRATION

I n 1939, Anne Clancy sat on a block of ice at the Mid City Pool in Menands. Being summer, she was wearing a bathing suit while her friend Alice Wills held an electric fan, an appliance that had exploded in use since mass manufacturing began in earnest more than a decade before. The photo (on page 149) is from 80 years ago, but it's essentially a modern image. The women's suits wouldn't look out of place in a 1970s snapshot; Clancy even has a bandage on one heel of a bare leg, perhaps from where the strap of a new summer sandal had chafed.

Recreation, or leisure-time pursuit, has at the root of its name "create," a verb traced to the Latin for "to produce." Unlike the output of most laborious toil for pay, amusements are an end until themselves: for the fun of playing a sport, of making music, of pulling pike from an iced-over pond in Grafton, of dressing for a parade to celebrate history, or of making a trip to Broadway in Saratoga Springs in June of 1936 in hopes of seeing Jean Harlow during filming of the movie *Saratoga*, which would become the second-highest-grossing film the following year, behind only *Snow White and the Seven Dwarfs*.

Central to the recreations of the past are those we continue to enjoy today, prominent among them is horse racing in the Spa City. Even in summer 2020, when conventional attendance at the Saratoga Race Course wasn't possible during the coronavirus pandemic, people found ways to gather to watch and play the ponies. The collective urge to commune and celebrate refuses to be thwarted. In a few years, for the 400th anniversary of the 1624 Dutch founding of the Albany predecessor of Fort Orange, one would wish for an extravaganza at least on par with the tricentennial of 1924, when a crowd of 15,000 spectators for a 60-float procession prompted the *Times Union* to proclaim it "the greatest parade the City had ever witnessed."

We can't, in the middle of the social withdrawal that is the coronavirus pandemic, say it will be so; it is difficult to project what has been lost, to both the scourge of disease and to the advancements of technology, which make it ever easier to be constantly connected and yet not actually together.

But hope remains, too: One cannot ice skate in Albany's Washington Park, or swim in Schenectady's Central Park or in Victoria Pool in the Saratoga Spa State Park, without actually going there, being there, doing it. The urge to create usually carries with it a desire to share.

Steve Barnes

OPPOSITE: Flag Day Parade, State Street, Albany, June 14, 1914. COURTESY ALBANY INSTITUTE OF HISTORY & ART

ABOVE: Hoosick Falls Citizens Corps Band under band leader Henderson Van Surdam in 1892. Formed in 1873, the band has been performing ever since, and, at the time of publication is known as the Hoosick Falls Community Band.
COURTESY HOOSICK TOWNSHIP HISTORICAL SOCIETY

ABOVE RIGHT: Backyard camping, Nassau, circa 1895. COURTESY VILLAGE OF NASSAU

RIGHT: Floral Fete, Saratoga Springs, circa 1890.
COURTESY SARATOGA SPRINGS PUBLIC LIBRARY

LEFT: Masons Temple Commandery marching north on Broadway at Maiden Lane, near Stanwix Hall in Albany, 1864. The Art Deco style James T. Foley United State Courthouse stands in this location at the time of publication. COURTESY ALBANY PUBLIC LIBRARY

BELOW: Horse racing at the Nassau Fair, 1900. Local breeders often ran their ponies for both bragging rights and an occasional friendly wager. The fair was created in 1892 on land leased from the Rensselaer County Agricultural and Liberal Arts Society, and was held until 1944. In later years after the fair closed the track was used for greyhound racing. COURTESY VILLAGE OF NASSAU

RIGHT: John E. Madden, William Collins Whitney, and Lord Derby are among the attendees at Saratoga Race Course, 1904. Saratoga's first Thoroughbred meet, a four-day event, was held one month after the Battle of Gettysburg, in August 1863. A group led by John Morrissey, William Travers, and Leonard Jerome purchased 125 acres of land and built a new grandstand to create Saratoga Race Course. The following year, a stakes race was named in honor of the first president of the track, William Travers, and it became the oldest stakes race for 3-year-old Thoroughbreds in the United States. The late 1800s were a time of decline for the track, but in 1901 an investment group, led by William Collins Whitney, purchased Saratoga Race Course. Major improvements were made, and the course earned back its good reputation. COURTESY NATIONAL MUSEUM OF RACING AND HALL OF FAME

OPPOSITE: Picnickers enjoying a summer excursion at J. N. Briggs's Baerena Park on Baeren Island in Coeymans, early 1900s. Located in the Hudson River 12 miles south of Albany, and accessible by steamboat ferry, the area was developed by businessman Briggs as a picnic area in 1879. With a covered dance platform, merry-go-round, refreshments, and an observation tower, it was a popular destination for group excursions of all sorts. The park even touted a Ferris wheel, added in 1893. COURTESY HARRY A. STURGES FOR RAVENA COEYMANS HISTORICAL SOCIETY

BELOW RIGHT: Holcomb's cornet band, Sand Lake, circa 1900. COURTESY SAND LAKE HISTORICAL SOCIETY

BELOW: L. A. Moure's Johnsonville Band, early 1900s. COURTESY PITTSTOWN HISTORICAL SOCIETY

RIGHT: A music float from the Floral Fete Parade in Saratoga Springs, 1901. Description from souvenir program reads: "A huge harp occupies nearly all the available space in this striking float. Garlands depend from every part of this enormous instrument, and two maskers, garbed in Greek robes, exert themselves to evoke harmonious sounds from the giant strings. In the front of the car an extraordinary plant grows, the leaves of which are in the form of violins and the blossoms in the form of trumpets. A slightly elevated compartment in the rear of the car is surrounded by a low parapet embellished with a bar of music and contains a group of musicians. A canopy shelters them from the sun."
COURTESY SARATOGA SPRINGS PUBLIC LIBRARY, NEW YORK HERITAGE DIGITAL COLLECTIONS

BELOW: Boating on Snyders Lake in North Greenbush, circa 1902.
COURTESY GREENBUSH HISTORICAL SOCIETY

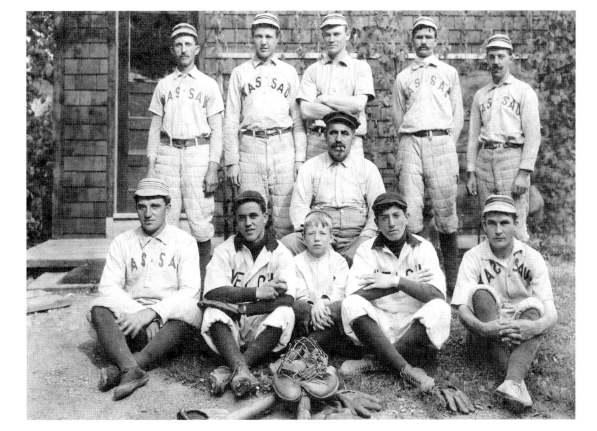

ABOVE: Replica of the *Half Moon* in the Hudson River at Albany during the Hudson-Fulton Celebration in 1909. The wooden sailing vessel was 85 feet long, square-rigged, and sported three masts. It could carry a crew of 15 to 20. COURTESY ALBANY PUBLIC LIBRARY

ABOVE LEFT: Workers from the Spier Falls Dam enjoying a card game in the Moreau and South Glens Falls area, circa 1902.
COURTESY PARKS-BENTLEY PLACE, HISTORICAL SOCIETY OF MOREAU AND SOUTH GLENS FALLS

LEFT: Nassau's "boys of summer" baseball team, 1902. Nassau has a long history of men's baseball teams, who often traveled as far as 30 miles for games. COURTESY VILLAGE OF NASSAU

The "Living Flag" at the Hudson-Fulton Celebration in Albany, 1909. The Hudson-Fulton Celebration was held from September 25 through October 2, 1909. Towns along the Hudson River celebrated the tercentenary of the discovery of the Hudson River and the centenary of the invention of the steamboat by Robert Fulton.

COURTESY ALBANY PUBLIC LIBRARY

ABOVE: Skating Pond in Washington Park, Albany, 1912. COURTESY ALBANY INSTITUTE OF HISTORY & ART

LEFT: Old Home Week Parade marching up John Street in Hoosick Falls during the third week of August in 1911. Old Home Week was a one-time event celebrating the growth and development of the village "from primitive to advanced methods." COURTESY HOOSICK TOWNSHIP HISTORICAL SOCIETY

ABOVE: Swimming at Central Park in Schenectady, circa 1915. COURTESY NEW YORK STATE ARCHIVES

RIGHT: Carman baseball club posing in front of a house with a trophy, Schenectady County, 1915. COURTESY SCHENECTADY COUNTY HISTORICAL SOCIETY, NEW YORK HERITAGE DIGITAL COLLECTIONS

Members of the Mohawk Giants baseball team, Schenectady, 1913. Front row, from left: Dolph White, unidentified, unidentified, Phil Bradley, Rich Richardson, Bill Wernecke (owner and business manager), Henry Wernecke, Knucks James, Chappie Johnson, Arthur Malette, unidentified. Back row: unidentified, Frank Wickware (star pitcher), Big Bill Smith (assistant business manager), Ashby Dunbar, Harry Buckner (top hitter), Johnny Pugh. On the ground at front is the batboy, Pete Fox. On the roster but unidentified or absent from photo: Walter Ball, Jesse Bragg, B. Brown, Mike Brown, Floyd Lawyer, Bill Pierce, Hank Williams. The Mohawk Giants were formed by William "Bill" Wernecke in 1913, and were one of Negro League baseball's early great independent teams. The same year they were formed the Mohawks defeated an all-star team led by the Washington Senators' legendary pitcher Walter Johnson.

COURTESY SCHENECTADY COUNTY HISTORICAL SOCIETY, NEW YORK HERITAGE DIGITAL COLLECTIONS

LEFT: Using a "tip-up" to fish for pickerel on Long Pond (later became part of Grafton Lakes State Park) near Grafton, February 1919. Using the tip-up, the fishermen could leave bait suspended through a hole in the ice, and detect when a fish would strike. COURTESY NEW YORK STATE ARCHIVES

OPPOSITE TOP RIGHT: A gathering at the spring at Congress Park near Saratoga Springs, August 1918. COURTESY NEW YORK STATE ARCHIVES

OPPOSITE LEFT: Michael B. "Mickey" Hogan of Cohoes, circa 1918. Hogan was signed to the New York Giants baseball team in 1918 by legendary manager John McGraw. While he didn't play in the regular season for the Giants, he was a local pitching legend and continued to play baseball well into the 1930s. According to an article in Troy's *Times Record* upon his death in 1968, "[Hogan] was a native and lifelong communicant of St. Bernard's Church... His service in the fire department extended from 1923 until 1937 and he was a member of the police department from 1951 until his retirement in 1961. 'Mike' had the deserved reputation of being one of the best baseball pitchers in this area." COURTESY HOGAN FAMILY ARCHIVES

OPPOSITE BOTTOM RIGHT: World War I Red Cross float in the Decoration Day Parade, Bethlehem, 1916. COURTESY BETHLEHEM HISTORICAL ASSOCIATION

ABOVE: Memorial Day Parade in Eagle Mills, Brunswick, 1919.
COURTESY BRUNSWICK HISTORICAL SOCIETY

ABOVE RIGHT: A. C. Cheney baseball team, Village of Castleton-on-Hudson, circa 1920. Front row, from left: "Flop" Gardenier, Frank Shiel, George "Red" Armer, Francis Durkin, Frank Price, Charles Horendel, unidentified, George Smith, Albert Rorbach, John Conlin, James Ronin. Back row: Martin Miller, Harry Finkle, Louis Horton, Loy "Doll" Leonard, Jay Smith, A. C. Cheney, Frank Lunch, Almsted "Ump" Blythe, Walter Brockley, Martin Hoffman, Robert Blythe.
COURTESY VILLAGE OF CASTLETON-ON-HUDSON

RIGHT: Drinking mineral water from a fountain at the State Drink Hall, an establishment for the serving of mineral water on the New York State Reservation (later became Saratoga Spa State Park) near Saratoga Springs, fall 1918.
COURTESY NEW YORK STATE ARCHIVES

LEFT: Morvich (with jockey Albert Johnson up) and trainer Fred Burlew after winning the 1921 Hopeful Stakes at Saratoga Race Course. Established in 1904 and still held at the time of publication, the Hopeful Stakes is a race restricted to 2-year-old horses. It is unique in that it is named for a life outlook or attitude rather than in honor of a person, place, or horse. People are "hopeful" that these young and largely unproven 2-year-olds develop into special racehorses. It has been held every year at Saratoga Race Course, with two exceptions: It was not run at all in 1911 or 1912, as racing was banned in New York, and was held at Belmont Park from 1943 to 1945 due to travel restrictions during World War II.
COURTESY NATIONAL MUSEUM OF RACING AND HALL OF FAME

BELOW LEFT: Albany residents dressed for the Tercentenary Pageant on June 3, 1924. It was in grand style that the city marked the 300th anniversary of the establishment of Fort Orange. Albany stores and schools closed early for a 2 p.m. parade, which the *Times-Union* (the paper's name was hyphenated at that time) described as "the greatest parade the City had ever witnessed." In all, 15,000 people, 60 floats and 30 bands marched through the city. COURTESY ALBANY PUBLIC LIBRARY

Harold Cormie raising the American flag at the ceremonies commemorating the 1777 Battle of Saratoga on the Saratoga Battlefield in Stillwater, 1932.

Glenville Baseball Team, 1934.
COURTESY GLENVILLE HISTORY CENTER

ABOVE: A float in the Dongan Charter Celebration Parade in Albany, July 22, 1936. The celebration was held to commemorate the 250th anniversary of the signing of the city's charter by Governor Thomas Dongan in 1686, which turned the village of Albany into a city. COURTESY ALBANY PUBLIC LIBRARY

ABOVE LEFT: Nassau Boy's Bugle and Drum Corps, circa 1935. The group performed at social functions, parades, and field days. COURTESY VILLAGE OF NASSAU

OPPOSITE: Lee Arlen, a stand-in for actress Jean Harlow, sitting at the wheel of the big roadster in which she sped up and down Broadway during the filming of the movie *Saratoga*, June 16, 1936. Harlow died before filming was finished, and it had to be completed using stand-ins. *Saratoga* was MGM's biggest moneymaker of 1937 and became the second-highest grossing film of that year, second only to Walt Disney's *Snow White and the Seven Dwarfs*. COURTESY NEW YORK STATE ARCHIVES

LEFT Stillwater Blockhouse, 1937. The blockhouse was built in part with timbers from Revolutionary era structures on the Neilsen Farm, which stood within what later became Saratoga National Historical Park. It replicates the early 18th century blockhouses of the region, but was actually built in 1927 as New York State turned the Saratoga Battlefield into an historical park. The "Battlefield blockhouse" was used as a visitor center and museum. When a new visitors center was constructed by the National Park Service, it was donated in 1975 to the Town of Stillwater. At the time of publication the blockhouse sits in a small park on the Hudson River, and is dedicated to local history. COURTESY STILLWATER PUBLIC LIBRARY AND THE HISTORIAN'S OFFICE

ABOVE: The Petersburg Band in 1939. The turn of the 20th century saw a plethora of local bands.
COURTESY TOWN OF PETERSBURGH

ABOVE RIGHT: Women attending a fashion show thrown by *The Knickerbocker Press* at Capitol Theater in Albany, September 26, 1936. COURTESY TIMES UNION HISTORIC IMAGES

OPPOSITE: Anne Clancy and Alice Wills cooling off at Mid City Pool, Menands, 1939.
COURTESY ALBANY INSTITUTE OF HISTORY & ART

RIGHT: Pause with jockey G. Seabo up winning the first race at Saratoga Race Course on August 3, 1938.
COURTESY NATIONAL MUSEUM OF RACING AND HALL OF FAME

INDEX